50 Breakfast Salad Recipes

By: Kelly Johnson

Table of Contents

- Avocado and Poached Egg Salad
- Spinach and Bacon Breakfast Salad
- Tomato, Cucumber, and Feta Salad
- Arugula and Smoked Salmon Salad
- Kale and Quinoa Breakfast Salad
- Mixed Berry Salad with Yogurt Dressing
- Sweet Potato and Spinach Salad with Poached Eggs
- Greek Yogurt and Granola Salad
- Cantaloupe, Prosciutto, and Arugula Salad
- Roasted Beet and Goat Cheese Salad
- Avocado and Grapefruit Salad with Honey Vinaigrette
- Roasted Veggie Breakfast Salad with Eggs
- Apple and Almond Salad with Maple Dressing
- Shaved Carrot and Kale Salad
- Chia Seed and Banana Breakfast Salad
- Pear and Blue Cheese Salad with Walnuts
- Chicken and Avocado Salad with Lemon Dressing
- Tropical Mango and Coconut Salad
- Spinach and Egg Salad with Bacon
- Strawberry and Almond Salad with Balsamic Glaze
- Avocado and Tomato Salad with Cilantro
- Citrus Salad with Poppy Seed Dressing
- Sweet Potato, Kale, and Egg Salad
- Grilled Peach and Burrata Salad
- Watermelon and Mint Breakfast Salad
- Apple, Pecan, and Cranberry Salad
- Roasted Mushroom and Spinach Salad with Fried Egg
- Pomegranate and Almond Breakfast Salad
- Beetroot and Arugula Salad with Goat Cheese
- Radish and Cucumber Salad with Lemon Dressing
- Roasted Brussels Sprout and Bacon Salad
- Avocado, Tomato, and Cucumber Salad
- Chopped Salad with Eggs and Bacon
- Sweet Potato, Black Bean, and Kale Salad
- Avocado, Mango, and Cucumber Salad

- Spinach, Feta, and Walnut Salad
- Mediterranean Breakfast Salad with Olives
- Berries, Spinach, and Almond Salad
- Roasted Asparagus and Egg Salad
- Cottage Cheese and Pineapple Salad
- Grilled Zucchini and Tomato Salad
- Apple and Walnut Salad with Cinnamon Dressing
- Eggplant and Tomato Salad with Yogurt Sauce
- Sliced Grapefruit and Arugula Salad
- Watermelon, Mint, and Feta Salad
- Roasted Sweet Potato and Arugula Salad
- Avocado, Chickpea, and Tomato Salad
- Ricotta and Fig Breakfast Salad
- Chilled Cucumber and Dill Salad
- Bacon, Avocado, and Spinach Salad

Avocado and Poached Egg Salad

Ingredients:

- 1 ripe avocado, sliced
- 2 poached eggs
- 2 cups mixed greens (arugula, spinach, or your choice)
- 1/4 cup cherry tomatoes, halved
- 1/4 red onion, thinly sliced
- 1 tbsp olive oil
- 1 tsp lemon juice
- Salt and pepper, to taste

Instructions:

1. On a plate, arrange the mixed greens, cherry tomatoes, and red onion.
2. Place the sliced avocado and poached eggs on top of the salad.
3. Drizzle with olive oil and lemon juice, then season with salt and pepper.
4. Serve immediately for a fresh and nutritious breakfast or brunch.

Spinach and Bacon Breakfast Salad

Ingredients:

- 2 cups fresh spinach
- 2 slices cooked bacon, crumbled
- 1/4 cup sliced mushrooms
- 1/4 cup shredded cheese (cheddar or your choice)
- 1 tbsp olive oil
- 1 tsp balsamic vinegar
- Salt and pepper, to taste

Instructions:

1. In a bowl, toss the spinach, mushrooms, and crumbled bacon together.
2. Drizzle with olive oil and balsamic vinegar, then season with salt and pepper.
3. Sprinkle with shredded cheese.
4. Serve as a savory, satisfying breakfast or side salad.

Tomato, Cucumber, and Feta Salad

Ingredients:

- 1 large tomato, diced
- 1 cucumber, peeled and sliced
- 1/4 cup crumbled feta cheese
- 2 tbsp olive oil
- 1 tbsp red wine vinegar
- Salt and pepper, to taste
- Fresh basil leaves, for garnish

Instructions:

1. In a bowl, combine the tomato, cucumber, and feta cheese.
2. Drizzle with olive oil and red wine vinegar, and toss gently to coat.
3. Season with salt and pepper, and garnish with fresh basil.
4. Serve as a refreshing, light breakfast or lunch.

Arugula and Smoked Salmon Salad

Ingredients:

- 2 cups fresh arugula
- 3 oz smoked salmon, torn into pieces
- 1/4 cup red onion, thinly sliced
- 1/2 tbsp capers
- 1 tbsp olive oil
- 1 tsp lemon juice
- Salt and pepper, to taste

Instructions:

1. On a platter, arrange the arugula, smoked salmon, and red onion slices.
2. Sprinkle with capers and drizzle with olive oil and lemon juice.
3. Season with salt and pepper.
4. Serve immediately for a quick and gourmet breakfast or brunch salad.

Kale and Quinoa Breakfast Salad

Ingredients:

- 2 cups kale, chopped
- 1/2 cup cooked quinoa
- 1/4 cup dried cranberries
- 1/4 cup chopped nuts (almonds or walnuts)
- 1 tbsp olive oil
- 1 tsp honey
- Salt and pepper, to taste

Instructions:

1. Massage the chopped kale with olive oil until it softens.
2. Add the cooked quinoa, cranberries, and chopped nuts to the kale.
3. Drizzle with honey, season with salt and pepper, and toss to combine.
4. Serve as a filling, nutrient-packed breakfast or salad.

Mixed Berry Salad with Yogurt Dressing

Ingredients:

- 1/2 cup strawberries, sliced
- 1/2 cup blueberries
- 1/2 cup raspberries
- 1/4 cup Greek yogurt
- 1 tbsp honey
- 1 tsp lemon juice
- Fresh mint leaves, for garnish
  Instructions:
1. In a bowl, combine the mixed berries.
2. In a small bowl, whisk together the Greek yogurt, honey, and lemon juice until smooth.
3. Drizzle the yogurt dressing over the berries, and toss gently.
4. Garnish with fresh mint leaves and serve as a sweet and tangy breakfast salad.

Sweet Potato and Spinach Salad with Poached Eggs

Ingredients:

- 1 small sweet potato, peeled and diced
- 2 cups fresh spinach
- 2 poached eggs
- 1 tbsp olive oil
- 1 tsp smoked paprika
- Salt and pepper, to taste

Instructions:

1. In a skillet, heat the olive oil over medium heat. Add the diced sweet potato and cook until tender, about 10-12 minutes.
2. In a bowl, toss the spinach and cooked sweet potato together.
3. Place the poached eggs on top and sprinkle with smoked paprika, salt, and pepper.
4. Serve immediately for a hearty and nutritious breakfast salad.

Greek Yogurt and Granola Salad

Ingredients:

- 1 cup Greek yogurt
- 1/4 cup granola
- 1/2 cup mixed fresh fruit (berries, banana, etc.)
- 1 tbsp honey
- 1/4 tsp cinnamon (optional)

Instructions:

1. In a bowl, scoop the Greek yogurt and top with granola and fresh fruit.
2. Drizzle with honey and sprinkle with cinnamon if desired.
3. Serve as a light and satisfying breakfast or snack.

Cantaloupe, Prosciutto, and Arugula Salad

Ingredients:

- 2 cups arugula
- 1/2 cantaloupe, sliced
- 4 slices prosciutto, torn into pieces
- 1/4 cup crumbled feta or goat cheese
- 1 tbsp olive oil
- 1 tsp balsamic vinegar
- Salt and pepper, to taste

Instructions:

1. Arrange the arugula on a plate and top with slices of cantaloupe and prosciutto.
2. Sprinkle with crumbled cheese and drizzle with olive oil and balsamic vinegar.
3. Season with salt and pepper, then serve immediately for a fresh and savory salad.

Roasted Beet and Goat Cheese Salad

Ingredients:

- 2 medium beets, peeled and cubed
- 2 cups mixed greens (spinach, arugula, etc.)
- 1/4 cup goat cheese, crumbled
- 1/4 cup walnuts, toasted
- 1 tbsp olive oil
- 1 tbsp balsamic vinegar
- Salt and pepper, to taste
  Instructions:

1. Preheat the oven to 400°F (200°C). Toss the beets with olive oil and season with salt and pepper. Roast for 25-30 minutes, until tender.
2. In a bowl, combine the roasted beets with mixed greens and top with goat cheese and walnuts.
3. Drizzle with balsamic vinegar and serve as a vibrant, earthy salad.

Avocado and Grapefruit Salad with Honey Vinaigrette

Ingredients:

- 1 ripe avocado, sliced
- 1 grapefruit, peeled and segmented
- 2 cups arugula
- 1 tbsp honey
- 1 tbsp olive oil
- 1 tsp lemon juice
- Salt and pepper, to taste

Instructions:

1. Arrange the arugula on a plate and top with avocado slices and grapefruit segments.
2. In a small bowl, whisk together the honey, olive oil, and lemon juice. Drizzle over the salad.
3. Season with salt and pepper, and serve immediately for a refreshing and tangy breakfast or brunch salad.

Roasted Veggie Breakfast Salad with Eggs

Ingredients:

- 1 cup roasted vegetables (sweet potato, bell pepper, zucchini)
- 2 poached eggs
- 2 cups spinach or mixed greens
- 1 tbsp olive oil
- Salt and pepper, to taste
  Instructions:
1. Roast the vegetables at 400°F (200°C) for 20-25 minutes, until tender.
2. Toss the roasted vegetables with spinach or mixed greens.
3. Top with poached eggs, drizzle with olive oil, and season with salt and pepper.
4. Serve warm for a hearty, nutrient-packed breakfast salad.

Apple and Almond Salad with Maple Dressing

Ingredients:

- 1 apple, thinly sliced
- 2 cups mixed greens (arugula, spinach, etc.)
- 1/4 cup sliced almonds, toasted
- 1 tbsp maple syrup
- 1 tbsp olive oil
- 1 tsp Dijon mustard
- Salt and pepper, to taste

Instructions:

1. In a small bowl, whisk together maple syrup, olive oil, Dijon mustard, salt, and pepper.
2. Toss the mixed greens with apple slices and toasted almonds.
3. Drizzle with the maple dressing and serve immediately as a sweet and crunchy salad.

Shaved Carrot and Kale Salad

Ingredients:

- 2 cups kale, finely chopped
- 2 medium carrots, peeled and shaved
- 1/4 cup pumpkin seeds
- 1 tbsp olive oil
- 1 tbsp apple cider vinegar
- Salt and pepper, to taste
  Instructions:
1. In a bowl, toss the kale and carrot ribbons together.
2. Drizzle with olive oil and apple cider vinegar, then season with salt and pepper.
3. Sprinkle with pumpkin seeds and serve as a fresh, vitamin-rich salad.

Chia Seed and Banana Breakfast Salad

Ingredients:

- 1 ripe banana, sliced
- 2 tbsp chia seeds
- 1/2 cup Greek yogurt
- 1 tbsp honey
- 1/4 tsp cinnamon

Instructions:

1. In a bowl, layer the sliced banana and chia seeds.
2. Top with Greek yogurt and drizzle with honey.
3. Sprinkle with cinnamon and serve immediately as a nutritious, filling breakfast.

Pear and Blue Cheese Salad with Walnuts

Ingredients:

- 1 ripe pear, sliced
- 2 cups mixed greens
- 1/4 cup blue cheese, crumbled
- 1/4 cup walnuts, toasted
- 1 tbsp olive oil
- 1 tbsp balsamic vinegar
- Salt and pepper, to taste

Instructions:

1. Arrange the mixed greens on a plate and top with pear slices, blue cheese, and toasted walnuts.
2. Drizzle with olive oil and balsamic vinegar, and season with salt and pepper.
3. Serve immediately for a sweet and savory salad perfect for brunch or lunch.

Chicken and Avocado Salad with Lemon Dressing

Ingredients:

- 2 cups mixed greens
- 1 cooked chicken breast, sliced
- 1 ripe avocado, sliced
- 1/4 cup cherry tomatoes, halved
- 1/4 cup red onion, thinly sliced
- 1 tbsp olive oil
- 1 tbsp lemon juice
- Salt and pepper, to taste

Instructions:

1. Arrange the mixed greens on a plate and top with sliced chicken, avocado, cherry tomatoes, and red onion.
2. Drizzle with olive oil and lemon juice, then season with salt and pepper.
3. Toss gently and serve for a light, protein-packed salad.

Tropical Mango and Coconut Salad

Ingredients:

- 2 cups mixed greens
- 1 ripe mango, peeled and diced
- 1/4 cup shredded coconut
- 1/4 cup toasted cashews
- 1 tbsp lime juice
- 1 tbsp honey
- Salt, to taste

Instructions:

1. Combine the mixed greens, mango, coconut, and cashews in a bowl.
2. In a small bowl, whisk together lime juice, honey, and a pinch of salt.
3. Drizzle the dressing over the salad and toss gently. Serve immediately for a fresh tropical flavor.

Spinach and Egg Salad with Bacon

Ingredients:

- 2 cups fresh spinach
- 2 hard-boiled eggs, sliced
- 3 slices bacon, cooked and crumbled
- 1/4 cup cherry tomatoes, halved
- 1 tbsp olive oil
- 1 tbsp red wine vinegar
- Salt and pepper, to taste

Instructions:

1. Toss spinach, egg slices, bacon, and cherry tomatoes in a bowl.
2. Drizzle with olive oil and red wine vinegar, and season with salt and pepper.
3. Gently mix and serve as a hearty breakfast or lunch salad.

Strawberry and Almond Salad with Balsamic Glaze

Ingredients:

- 2 cups mixed greens
- 1 cup fresh strawberries, sliced
- 1/4 cup sliced almonds, toasted
- 1 tbsp olive oil
- 1 tbsp balsamic vinegar
- 1 tbsp honey
- Salt and pepper, to taste

Instructions:

1. Arrange the mixed greens on a plate and top with sliced strawberries and toasted almonds.
2. In a small bowl, whisk together olive oil, balsamic vinegar, honey, salt, and pepper.
3. Drizzle the balsamic glaze over the salad and serve immediately for a sweet and tangy salad.

Avocado and Tomato Salad with Cilantro

Ingredients:

- 2 ripe avocados, sliced
- 1 cup cherry tomatoes, halved
- 1/4 cup red onion, finely chopped
- 1/4 cup fresh cilantro, chopped
- 1 tbsp olive oil
- 1 tbsp lime juice
- Salt and pepper, to taste

Instructions:

1. Combine the avocado slices, cherry tomatoes, and red onion in a bowl.
2. Drizzle with olive oil and lime juice, then sprinkle with cilantro, salt, and pepper.
3. Toss gently and serve for a refreshing, creamy salad.

Citrus Salad with Poppy Seed Dressing

Ingredients:

- 1 orange, peeled and segmented
- 1 grapefruit, peeled and segmented
- 1 cup mixed greens
- 1 tbsp poppy seeds
- 2 tbsp honey
- 1 tbsp lemon juice
- 1 tbsp olive oil
- Salt, to taste
  Instructions:
1. Arrange the citrus segments and mixed greens on a plate.
2. In a small bowl, whisk together poppy seeds, honey, lemon juice, olive oil, and salt.
3. Drizzle the dressing over the citrus salad and serve immediately for a bright and tangy dish.

Sweet Potato, Kale, and Egg Salad

Ingredients:

- 2 cups kale, chopped
- 1 medium sweet potato, roasted and cubed
- 2 hard-boiled eggs, sliced
- 1/4 cup pumpkin seeds
- 1 tbsp olive oil
- 1 tbsp apple cider vinegar
- Salt and pepper, to taste

Instructions:

1. Toss the kale, roasted sweet potato, and egg slices together in a bowl.
2. Sprinkle with pumpkin seeds and drizzle with olive oil and apple cider vinegar.
3. Season with salt and pepper, then serve as a warm, nutritious salad.

Grilled Peach and Burrata Salad

Ingredients:

- 2 peaches, halved and pitted
- 2 cups arugula
- 1 ball burrata cheese
- 1 tbsp honey
- 1 tbsp balsamic vinegar
- 1 tbsp olive oil
- Salt and pepper, to taste
  Instructions:
1. Grill the peach halves for 2-3 minutes on each side until slightly charred.
2. Arrange the arugula on a plate and top with grilled peaches and burrata cheese.
3. Drizzle with honey, balsamic vinegar, and olive oil, then season with salt and pepper.
4. Serve immediately for a sweet and savory summer salad.

Watermelon and Mint Breakfast Salad

Ingredients:

- 2 cups cubed watermelon
- 1/4 cup fresh mint leaves, chopped
- 1 tbsp lime juice
- 1 tsp honey (optional)
- 1/4 cup crumbled feta cheese (optional)

Instructions:

1. Combine the cubed watermelon and chopped mint in a bowl.
2. Drizzle with lime juice and honey (if using).
3. Toss gently and top with feta cheese for a refreshing, sweet, and savory salad.

Apple, Pecan, and Cranberry Salad

Ingredients:

- 2 cups mixed greens
- 1 apple, thinly sliced
- 1/4 cup pecans, toasted
- 1/4 cup dried cranberries
- 1 tbsp olive oil
- 1 tbsp apple cider vinegar
- Salt and pepper, to taste

Instructions:

1. Toss the mixed greens, apple slices, toasted pecans, and dried cranberries together in a bowl.
2. Drizzle with olive oil and apple cider vinegar, then season with salt and pepper.
3. Toss gently and serve as a light and sweet breakfast or side salad.

Roasted Mushroom and Spinach Salad with Fried Egg

Ingredients:

- 1 cup roasted mushrooms (button or cremini)
- 2 cups spinach, fresh
- 1 egg, fried
- 1 tbsp olive oil
- Salt and pepper, to taste
- 1 tbsp balsamic vinegar

Instructions:

1. Toss the roasted mushrooms and spinach in a bowl.
2. Drizzle with olive oil and balsamic vinegar, and season with salt and pepper.
3. Top with the fried egg for a savory breakfast salad.

Pomegranate and Almond Breakfast Salad

Ingredients:

- 1 cup mixed greens
- 1/2 cup pomegranate seeds
- 1/4 cup almonds, sliced
- 1 tbsp olive oil
- 1 tbsp honey
- 1 tsp lemon juice

Instructions:

1. Combine the mixed greens, pomegranate seeds, and sliced almonds in a bowl.
2. Drizzle with olive oil, honey, and lemon juice.
3. Toss gently and serve for a fruity and crunchy salad.

Beetroot and Arugula Salad with Goat Cheese

Ingredients:

- 2 cups arugula
- 1/2 cup cooked beetroot, sliced
- 1/4 cup goat cheese, crumbled
- 1 tbsp olive oil
- 1 tbsp balsamic vinegar
- Salt and pepper, to taste

Instructions:

1. Toss the arugula and beetroot slices in a bowl.
2. Drizzle with olive oil and balsamic vinegar, then season with salt and pepper.
3. Top with crumbled goat cheese and serve for a light, earthy salad.

Radish and Cucumber Salad with Lemon Dressing

Ingredients:

- 1/2 cup radishes, thinly sliced
- 1/2 cup cucumber, thinly sliced
- 1 tbsp lemon juice
- 1 tbsp olive oil
- Salt and pepper, to taste
- Fresh dill (optional)

Instructions:

1. Combine the radishes and cucumber in a bowl.
2. In a separate bowl, whisk together lemon juice, olive oil, salt, and pepper.
3. Drizzle the dressing over the vegetables and toss. Garnish with fresh dill if desired. Serve immediately for a crisp, refreshing salad.

Roasted Brussels Sprout and Bacon Salad

Ingredients:

- 2 cups Brussels sprouts, halved and roasted
- 3 slices bacon, cooked and crumbled
- 1 tbsp olive oil
- 1 tbsp apple cider vinegar
- Salt and pepper, to taste
- 1/4 cup shaved Parmesan cheese (optional)

Instructions:

1. Toss the roasted Brussels sprouts and crumbled bacon in a bowl.
2. Drizzle with olive oil and apple cider vinegar, then season with salt and pepper.
3. Top with shaved Parmesan cheese and serve immediately for a savory and satisfying salad.

Avocado, Tomato, and Cucumber Salad

Ingredients:

- 1 avocado, diced
- 1 tomato, chopped
- 1/2 cucumber, sliced
- 1 tbsp olive oil
- 1 tsp lemon juice
- Salt and pepper, to taste
- Fresh basil leaves, chopped (optional)

Instructions:

1. Combine the diced avocado, chopped tomato, and sliced cucumber in a bowl.
2. Drizzle with olive oil and lemon juice, then season with salt and pepper.
3. Toss gently and garnish with fresh basil leaves for a light and refreshing salad.

Chopped Salad with Eggs and Bacon

Ingredients:

- 2 hard-boiled eggs, chopped
- 2 slices bacon, cooked and crumbled
- 2 cups mixed greens
- 1/4 cup cherry tomatoes, halved
- 1/4 cup cucumber, chopped
- 1 tbsp olive oil
- 1 tbsp red wine vinegar
- Salt and pepper, to taste

Instructions:

1. In a large bowl, combine the chopped eggs, crumbled bacon, mixed greens, cherry tomatoes, and cucumber.
2. Drizzle with olive oil and red wine vinegar, and season with salt and pepper.
3. Toss gently and serve for a hearty, protein-packed salad.

Sweet Potato, Black Bean, and Kale Salad

Ingredients:

- 1 medium sweet potato, cubed and roasted
- 1 cup black beans, cooked
- 2 cups kale, chopped
- 1 tbsp olive oil
- 1 tbsp lime juice
- 1/2 tsp cumin
- Salt and pepper, to taste
- Fresh cilantro, chopped (optional)
  Instructions:

1. Toss the roasted sweet potato cubes, black beans, and chopped kale in a bowl.
2. Drizzle with olive oil and lime juice, and season with cumin, salt, and pepper.
3. Garnish with fresh cilantro if desired and serve for a filling and nutritious salad.

Avocado, Mango, and Cucumber Salad

Ingredients:

- 1 avocado, diced
- 1 mango, peeled and diced
- 1/2 cucumber, sliced
- 1 tbsp lime juice
- 1 tbsp olive oil
- Salt and pepper, to taste
- Fresh mint, chopped (optional)

Instructions:

1. Combine the diced avocado, mango, and cucumber in a bowl.
2. Drizzle with lime juice and olive oil, then season with salt and pepper.
3. Toss gently and garnish with fresh mint for a tropical and refreshing salad.

Spinach, Feta, and Walnut Salad

Ingredients:

- 2 cups fresh spinach
- 1/4 cup feta cheese, crumbled
- 1/4 cup walnuts, toasted
- 1 tbsp olive oil
- 1 tbsp balsamic vinegar
- Salt and pepper, to taste

Instructions:

1. In a bowl, toss the spinach, crumbled feta, and toasted walnuts.
2. Drizzle with olive oil and balsamic vinegar, then season with salt and pepper.
3. Toss gently and serve for a light, savory salad.

Mediterranean Breakfast Salad with Olives

Ingredients:

- 2 cups mixed greens
- 1/4 cup Kalamata olives, pitted and sliced
- 1/4 cup cherry tomatoes, halved
- 1/4 cucumber, sliced
- 1 tbsp olive oil
- 1 tbsp lemon juice
- Salt and pepper, to taste
- Feta cheese, crumbled (optional)

Instructions:

1. Combine the mixed greens, olives, cherry tomatoes, and cucumber in a bowl.
2. Drizzle with olive oil and lemon juice, then season with salt and pepper.
3. Top with crumbled feta cheese if desired and toss gently. Serve for a Mediterranean-inspired breakfast.

Berries, Spinach, and Almond Salad

Ingredients:

- 2 cups fresh spinach
- 1/2 cup mixed berries (strawberries, blueberries, raspberries)
- 1/4 cup sliced almonds, toasted
- 1 tbsp honey
- 1 tbsp balsamic vinegar
- Salt and pepper, to taste

Instructions:

1. Toss the spinach, mixed berries, and toasted almonds in a bowl.
2. Drizzle with honey and balsamic vinegar, and season with salt and pepper.
3. Toss gently and serve for a sweet and nutritious breakfast salad.

Roasted Asparagus and Egg Salad

Ingredients:

- 1 bunch asparagus, trimmed and roasted
- 2 hard-boiled eggs, chopped
- 2 cups mixed greens
- 1 tbsp olive oil
- 1 tbsp lemon juice
- Salt and pepper, to taste

Instructions:

1. Combine the roasted asparagus, chopped eggs, and mixed greens in a bowl.
2. Drizzle with olive oil and lemon juice, then season with salt and pepper.
3. Toss gently and serve for a savory and satisfying breakfast salad.

Cottage Cheese and Pineapple Salad

Ingredients:

- 1 cup cottage cheese
- 1/2 cup pineapple chunks, fresh or canned
- 1 tbsp honey (optional)
- 1 tbsp chopped fresh mint (optional)

Instructions:

1. In a bowl, combine the cottage cheese and pineapple chunks.
2. Drizzle with honey for added sweetness, if desired.
3. Garnish with fresh mint and serve chilled for a light, refreshing salad.

Grilled Zucchini and Tomato Salad

Ingredients:

- 2 medium zucchinis, sliced into rounds
- 1 cup cherry tomatoes, halved
- 1 tbsp olive oil
- 1 tsp balsamic vinegar
- Salt and pepper, to taste
- Fresh basil leaves, chopped (optional)

Instructions:

1. Heat the grill or a grill pan over medium heat.
2. Toss the zucchini slices with olive oil, salt, and pepper, and grill for 3-4 minutes per side, until tender and lightly charred.
3. In a bowl, combine the grilled zucchini with halved cherry tomatoes.
4. Drizzle with balsamic vinegar and toss gently.
5. Garnish with fresh basil, if desired, and serve warm or at room temperature.

Apple and Walnut Salad with Cinnamon Dressing

Ingredients:

- 2 apples, cored and sliced
- 1/4 cup walnuts, toasted
- 2 cups mixed greens
- 1 tbsp olive oil
- 1 tbsp apple cider vinegar
- 1/2 tsp cinnamon
- 1 tsp honey
- Salt and pepper, to taste

Instructions:

1. In a small bowl, whisk together the olive oil, apple cider vinegar, cinnamon, honey, salt, and pepper to make the dressing.
2. In a large bowl, toss the apple slices, toasted walnuts, and mixed greens.
3. Drizzle with the cinnamon dressing and toss to coat.
4. Serve immediately for a sweet and savory salad.

Eggplant and Tomato Salad with Yogurt Sauce

Ingredients:

- 1 medium eggplant, cubed
- 1 cup cherry tomatoes, halved
- 1/2 cup plain Greek yogurt
- 1 tbsp olive oil
- 1 tbsp lemon juice
- 1 garlic clove, minced
- Salt and pepper, to taste
- Fresh parsley, chopped (optional)

Instructions:

1. Heat the olive oil in a pan over medium heat. Add the cubed eggplant and sauté for about 5-7 minutes, until soft and golden brown.
2. In a small bowl, mix together the Greek yogurt, lemon juice, minced garlic, salt, and pepper to create the yogurt sauce.
3. In a serving dish, combine the sautéed eggplant and halved cherry tomatoes.
4. Drizzle with the yogurt sauce and toss gently.
5. Garnish with fresh parsley if desired and serve warm or chilled.

Sliced Grapefruit and Arugula Salad

Ingredients:

- 2 grapefruits, peeled and sliced
- 2 cups arugula
- 1 tbsp olive oil
- 1 tsp honey
- Salt and pepper, to taste
- 1/4 cup goat cheese, crumbled (optional)

Instructions:

1. In a bowl, toss together the sliced grapefruit and arugula.
2. In a small bowl, whisk together the olive oil, honey, salt, and pepper.
3. Drizzle the dressing over the salad and toss gently to coat.
4. Top with crumbled goat cheese, if desired, and serve immediately for a tangy and refreshing salad.

Watermelon, Mint, and Feta Salad

Ingredients:

- 3 cups watermelon, cubed
- 1/4 cup crumbled feta cheese
- 1 tbsp fresh mint, chopped
- 1 tbsp olive oil
- 1 tbsp lime juice
- Salt and pepper, to taste

Instructions:

1. In a bowl, combine the cubed watermelon and crumbled feta cheese.
2. Drizzle with olive oil and lime juice, then season with salt and pepper.
3. Garnish with chopped fresh mint and serve chilled for a refreshing summer salad.

Roasted Sweet Potato and Arugula Salad

Ingredients:

- 2 medium sweet potatoes, peeled and cubed
- 2 tbsp olive oil
- Salt and pepper, to taste
- 4 cups arugula
- 1/4 cup goat cheese, crumbled
- 1/4 cup pumpkin seeds (optional)
- 1 tbsp balsamic vinegar

Instructions:

1. Preheat the oven to 400°F (200°C).
2. Toss the sweet potato cubes with olive oil, salt, and pepper. Spread them out on a baking sheet and roast for 20-25 minutes, or until tender and slightly caramelized.
3. In a large bowl, combine the roasted sweet potatoes, arugula, crumbled goat cheese, and pumpkin seeds.
4. Drizzle with balsamic vinegar and toss gently. Serve warm or at room temperature.

Avocado, Chickpea, and Tomato Salad

Ingredients:

- 1 ripe avocado, diced
- 1 cup chickpeas, cooked or canned, drained
- 1 cup cherry tomatoes, halved
- 1/4 cup red onion, thinly sliced
- 1 tbsp olive oil
- 1 tbsp lemon juice
- Salt and pepper, to taste
- Fresh parsley, chopped (optional)

Instructions:

1. In a large bowl, combine the diced avocado, chickpeas, cherry tomatoes, and red onion.
2. Drizzle with olive oil and lemon juice, then season with salt and pepper.
3. Gently toss the salad to combine.
4. Garnish with fresh parsley, if desired, and serve chilled or at room temperature.

Ricotta and Fig Breakfast Salad

Ingredients:

- 1/2 cup ricotta cheese
- 4-5 fresh figs, sliced
- 1 cup mixed greens
- 1 tbsp honey
- 1 tbsp lemon juice
- Fresh mint leaves (optional)

Instructions:

1. In a bowl, toss the mixed greens with lemon juice and honey.
2. Arrange the ricotta cheese, sliced figs, and greens on a plate.
3. Drizzle with extra honey if desired, and garnish with fresh mint leaves. Serve immediately for a light, nutritious breakfast salad.

Chilled Cucumber and Dill Salad

Ingredients:

- 2 medium cucumbers, thinly sliced
- 1/4 cup red onion, thinly sliced
- 2 tbsp fresh dill, chopped
- 1 tbsp white wine vinegar
- 1 tbsp olive oil
- Salt and pepper, to taste
- 1/4 cup Greek yogurt (optional)

Instructions:

1. In a bowl, combine the cucumber slices, red onion, and fresh dill.
2. Drizzle with white wine vinegar and olive oil, then season with salt and pepper.
3. Toss the salad gently to coat.
4. If desired, mix in Greek yogurt for extra creaminess. Serve chilled for a refreshing and light salad.

Bacon, Avocado, and Spinach Salad

Ingredients:

- 4 strips bacon, cooked and crumbled
- 2 cups spinach leaves
- 1 avocado, diced
- 1/4 cup red onion, thinly sliced
- 1 tbsp olive oil
- 1 tbsp balsamic vinegar
- Salt and pepper, to taste

Instructions:

1. In a large bowl, combine the spinach leaves, diced avocado, red onion, and crumbled bacon.
2. Drizzle with olive oil and balsamic vinegar, then season with salt and pepper.
3. Toss gently to combine. Serve immediately for a rich and satisfying salad.

www.ingramcontent.com/pod-product-compliance
Lightning Source LLC
LaVergne TN
LVHW081332060526
838201LV00055B/2593